REVEALED SECRETS OF THE TAROT

EDWIN J. NIGG

W. Foulsham & Co. Ltd.
London • New York • Toronto • Cape Town • Sydney

W. Foulsham & Company Limited
Yeovil Road, Slough, Berkshire, SL1 4JH

ISBN 0–572–01396–5

Originally published by Falken-Verlag GmbH
Niedernhausen/Ts, West Germany

Photographs copyright © 1986 Falken-Verlag

This English language edition copyright©1986
W. Foulsham & Co. Ltd

Reproduction of Tarot cards courtesy of U.S. Games Systems Inc.

All rights reserved.
The Copyright Act (1956) prohibits (subject to
certain very limited exceptions) the making of
copies of any copyright work or of a
substantial part of such a work, including the
making of copies by photocopying or similar
process. Written permission to make a copy
or copies must therefore normally be obtained
from the publisher in advance. It is advisable
also to consult the publisher if in any doubt
as to the legality of any copying which is to
be undertaken.

Printed in Great Britain by St Edmunsbury
Press, Bury St. Edmunds.

CONTENTS

INTRODUCTION 4
THE TAROT 5
TAROT AS A MEDIUM OF DIVINATION 15
THE CELTIC CROSS SPREAD 20
THE MAJOR ARCANA 24
THREE SAMPLE SPREADS 68
THE MINOR ARCANA 77
THE SPREAD ROWS OF SEVEN 87
THREE SAMPLE SPREADS AND THEIR READINGS 89

INTRODUCTION

This book is not a treatise on all aspects and the complete background of the Tarot. Tarot is a world in itself, an almost irreplaceable treasure which has survived for centuries without losing the slightest relevance. This book concentrates on predictions with Tarot cards, which is a complex and fascinating field in itself. Those who want to proceed further can go on to study the complex significance of the complete Tarot.

For a thoughtful person, it is a great challenge to illuminate his or her past by means of the Tarot cards, to enlighten the present and to project the sum of these insights onto the future. The Tarot cards undeniably offer the impetus necessary for such an undertaking – but without any doubts, simple fortune-telling is dangerous. Tarot cards are pictures laden with symbols which come to life only through our thoughts. Their purpose is to guide our reflections, to make us contemplate thoughts which we usually prefer to push aside.

Do not regard the Tarot as a mere card game – there is more to them, and by denying this, their significance is denied. But beware of placing too much importance on their messages. Cards in themselves are useless: they are brought to life through the reader's competence and concentration; they are filled with life through the reader's effort to feel with the seeker's personality.

I hope I will have succeeded in offering you an insight into the mysterious world of the Tarot. And if the cards occasionally help you in coping with your everyday problems, my trouble will have been worthwhile.

THE TAROT

In 1781, Court de Gebelin wrote in *Monde primitif*:

'Imagine the surprise it would cause if an old Egyptian book were re-discovered, a book from ancient Egypt which had been spared from the flames in the blazes of famous libraries and which contained the clearest and most profound knowledge of the ancient Egyptians. Certainly everybody would be keenly interested to learn of the mysteries of such an exceptional book. Now, would I not surprise you if I maintained that this book had never been lost, and that it had been in use for a very long time now in most parts of Europe and had been found in the hands of nearly everybody. Most surprising, however, would be if it was assured that nobody ever guessed it to be Egyptian, that one owned it without knowing, that hardly anyone had ever tried to decipher a single leaf, and that this fruit of exceptional wisdom was regarded to be a heap of extravagant figures which in themselves were meaningless.

'As a matter of fact, this Egyptian creation is the only one to have survived after all the other treasures and their knowledge were lost from Egyptian libraries. It became so popular that no sage ever deemed it worthy to ponder on its origins. Nobody apart from myself has done it. The book consist of 77, or rather 78 leaves, or pictures, which are divided into five groups. Each group reveals different amusing and instructive objects. In a word, it is the Tarot, a game not known in today's Paris, but very common in Italy, in Germany, and in the Provence. Of course, the game is bizarre, not only because of its strange figures and the large number of cards.'

TAROT CARDS

Tarot is the strangest, most unique of all card games. Already the cards' shape is exceptional, being about 110 mm long and 55 to 65 mm wide.

Strange, too, is the number of cards – there are 78 in every deck of Tarot cards, consisting of 22 Major and 56 Minor Arcana. The name 'Arcana' comes from the Latin and means 'Bearer of secrets', and indeed, each card does bear a secret.

THE MAJOR ARCANA

The Major Arcana show peculiar, scurrilous pictures and – apart from the first one which can be numbered 1, 22 or not at all – Roman numbers.

1, 22, or 0	Le Mat	The Fool
I	Le Bateleur	The Magician
II	Junon	The High Priestess
III	L'Imperatrice	The Empress
IIII	L'Empereur	The Emperor
V	Jupiter	The Hierophant
VI	L'Amoureux	The Lovers
VII	Le Chariot	The Chariot
VIII	La Justice	Justice
VIIII	L'Ermite	The Hermit
X	La Roue de Fortune	The Wheel of Fortune
XI	La Force	Strength
XII	Le Pendu	The Hanged Man
XIII	La Mort	Death
XIIII	Temperance	Temperance
XV	Le Diable	The Devil

XVI	La Maison de Dieu	The Tower
XVII	L'Etoile	The Star
XVIII	La Lune	The Moon
XVIIII	Le Soleil	The Sun
XX	Le Jugement	Judgment
XXI	Le Monde	The World

(In some packs, cards VIII and XI change positions.)

THE MINOR ARCANA

The Minor Arcana are made up of the same cards as any deck of cards, with the exception of the Knights. The old, now forgotten tradition of the Ace being equal to number one, i.e. the lowest card, was retained in the Tarot. Nor do the four suits correspond to our usual cards. In the Tarot, there are:

Swords (= Spades) Air
Wands (= Clubs) Fire
Cups (= Hearts) Water
Pentacles (= Diamonds) Earth

Each sequence consists of: King; Queen; Knight; Page; Ten; Nine; Eight; Seven; Six; Five; Four; Three; Two; One (= Ace).

THE ORIGIN OF THE TAROT

The actual origin of the Tarot is unknown. For centuries, books have been written on the Tarot, and for centuries, people have tried to solve the mystery of its origin. Whole libraries have been written on this topic. The most bizarre theories were developed and rejected, and yet still no scholar ever succeeded in establishing conclusive proofs for the beginnings of the Tarot.

It certainly would be wrong to claim that the Tarot was a card game like any other game. The confusing 22 Major Arcana and their decidedly strange figures, and the centuries old tradition of the Tarot defy any such attempts. I doubt, however, whether the Tarot can be regarded as the 'mother of all card games'.

Many people deny that the Tarot is a card game at all. It is regarded rather as a collection of mystic pictures of an ancient belief. But this theory will only hold for the 22 Major Arcana. The fact that these pictures were published again and again as playing cards does not support this suggestion.

But it is more profitable to deal with the known facts than linger over the mysterious origin of the Tarot.

The Italian Tarots

The Tarocchino di Bologna belong to the oldest Tarot cards. François Fibbia, Prince of Pisa, is said to have introduced these cards to his exile in Bologna. He died in 1419. The Tarocchino di Bologna consisted of 62 cards and were divided in exactly the same way as the Tarot decks we know today. Only the card numbers 2, 3, 4 and 5 of the Minor Arcana were missing.

One of the oldest Tarot decks still known today is the one by Visconti Sforza. It dates back to the years 1432–1466, and a few copies are still in existence. The deck is made up of truly superb cards of a very large size. The pictures are painted by hand and filled with rich details. The individual figures, though obviously painted in the style of the time, do not differ at all from the pictures which we know and use today. However, the two cards 'Junon' and 'Jupiter' are replaced by 'La Papesse' and 'Le Pape'.

These Italian Tarot cards are the earliest actual record of the Tarot. There are indications that the cards were known in previous centuries, but we know for sure that Tarot cards did exist in Italy from the middle of the 15th century.

What makes the Tarot so fascinating is the fact that the same cards have been produced now for more than 500 years, that the 22 Major Arcana have been depicting the same symbolic images for more than 500 years and that the significance, the validity and the contents of each card have not changed in that time. Should not this old tradition give a set-down even to the most convinced opponents of divination by means of the Tarot cards? It seems short of impossible that a tradition as complex as this could have survived half a millenium, had the cards not contained a fair amount of meaning and effect.

Tarot de Marseille

In the 18th century, a new kind of Tarot emerged from the dark: the Tarot de Marseille, and these cards are still the most popular ones in France. Court de Gebelin, a man with great knowledge of the Tarot, endeavoured not only to draw connections between the Tarot de Marseille and the ancient Egyptian wisdoms, but also to prove them. And indeed, there are a great number of close connections to ancient Egypt and the Book of Thoth (Crownys Book on Tarot).

Later, Eliphas Levi and Oswald Wirth were particularly interested in the connections between the Cabala, the mediaeval Jewish mystic teaching, and the game of Tarot. In this instance, too, correspondence between the two systems can be demonstrated and proved. This whole field, however, is beyond the scope of this book.

Recent Tarots

Until the beginning of this century, it was mainly the Italian Tarots and the Tarot de Marseille which were being used, if in several variations. Today, the range of Tarot cards has vastly increased.

Especially since the mid-fifties, demand has risen everywhere. Young people's interest in the old wisdom of the Tarot has led to the development of more than 250 different Tarot packs, which have definitely enriched the old traditions. However, with modern artists illustrating the old images, quite a number of old Tarot symbols were lost or covered up. This book therefore uses the traditional Tarott 1JJ which, in its plain simplicity, belongs to the Italian Tarots and which holds all the important elements of the Tarot. We know that this deck was produced in its present form 400 years ago. Minor changes which occur on individual cards do not imply any new interpretations, but result from the fact that the producers of the cards were rarely interested closely in the Tarot and its wisdom and that generations of woodcutters and illustrators made these colourful pictures without being aware of their value and their inherent significance.

The Tarot 1JJ has spread all over the world. It is used in Australia and America as well as in Japan and Scandinavia. In order not to alter the character of these precious cards, the Swiss card manufacturers have consciously decided against inscribing the cards with names in different languages. Therefore the old images still bear the traditional names, written in medieaval French, such as 'La Roue de Fortune', 'Le Chariot' and so on.

THE GREAT MASTERS OF TAROT

Antoine Court de Gebelin was born in Nîmes in 1725. A pastor's son, he studied theology in Lausanne, but his special interest was mythology. In 1781, his famous book *Le Monde Primitif, Analysé et Comparé avec le Monde Moderne* was published. In this treatise, Gebelin dealt in detail with the knowledge of the Tarot. With his vast specialist knowledge he claims that the origins of the secrets of the Tarot are to be found in Egypt.

The professor of mathematics, Alliette, was one of Gebelin's successors. Under the pseudonym Etteilla he published a book *Manière de se Récréer avec le Jeu de Cartes Nommées Tarot* in 1783.

Contrary to Gebelin and Etteilla, who traced the Tarot back to Egypt, Eliphas Levi believed the cards to be of Hebrew origin. Levi was a philosopher, and his civil name was Alphonse Louis Constant, under which he worked as a Catholic priest. His most famous book is called *Dogme et Rituel de la Haute Magie*.

Gerard Encausse is the fourth of the great masters of Tarot. He lived from 1865 to 1917 and found public acclaim under the name of Papus. His book *Le Tarot des Bohemians* is still regarded as the best and most original source of the Tarot wisdoms.

THE DEVELOPMENT OF THE TAROT

In the 1550s, it was mainly the Italian nobility who devoted themselves to the Tarot; a few years later, however, these cards could already be found in the houses of the merchants and the common people.

The fascination of the card game itself, combined with the secrets of divination, made for a quick distribution. On several occasions, the State and the Church attempted to stop it from spreading, but to no avail. The same development took place in France. In the other countries, it was mainly the gypsies who spread the card game.

Quite often the cards ended up in the hands of people who did not really know what to do with them. In that case, the cards were occasionally divided – the 22 Major Arcana were put aside, and the people played a normal card game with the remaining 56 cards. These 56 cards differ from the usual Whist or Bridge deck only through the additional figure of the Knight.

From this fact, many card scientists derived that Tarot is the real mother of all card games. If one omits the Knights and adds the unnumerated card of the Fool as Joker, one has a proper deck of Bridge.

I, personally, do not find this theory very convincing since we know that other card games were mentioned much earlier. It is also difficult to imagine that the starting point for the development of card games as a whole would be with such an extensive deck of cards.

In the first third of our millenium, the playing card appeared and bridged the gap between chess, which is fairly exacting, and the mere games of chance with sticks or dice. The ingenious combination of thoughtful play and chance, of skill and gamble, started off on a victorious advance – within a very short time, the normal card game had conquered the whole of Europe. Even in the times of the mass media it is inconceivable that a game should spread so quickly.

But how about divination? It is only natural that the Tarot cards in those dark ages of superstition should have been used for divinatory purposes. Already in those days, the most diverse kinds of fortune-tellers existed. The 'serious' ones amongst them constructed highly complicated methods of layout and founded a proper Tarot science.

For the greater part, however, the revealing images of the Major Arcana were interpreted emotionally, according to the reader's intuition – then as much as now.

Just as the circles of the initiated opposed the Tarot in order to keep intact the purity of their own teaching, so the Church for a long time condemned the cards as the devil's tools. The history of card-makers often reads like a story of suffering. Again and again the cards were forbidden and the card-makers were told to devote themselves solely to their second branch of income – the production of saint's images. Roman card-makers were evicted from the Vatican, and the theory that they took revenge with the cards number II and V, 'La Papesse' and 'Il Papa', was never refuted.

Even in modern cards one does find these two figures of the Pope and Papess. The Church violently opposed the playing of cards in general, and the fact that the Tarot was used for divinatory purposes made matters worse. In fact, it is probable that it was exactly this persecution which helped towards spreading the game even further and faster.

THE CARD GAME

Not only are the origins of the Tarot complicated and difficult to understand, the name itself often is confusing. In Italy, the cards were called *Tarocci*, whereas in the French-speaking areas they were always referred to as *Tarot*. This name was gradually taken over by the English-speaking countries. In the German-speaking regions, the terms *Tarok* and *Tarock* developed.

But the game using Tarot cards was not only attributed different names, one name meant, and often still does, various games. The Austian *Tarok*, also known as *coffee-house Tarok*, has just as little to do with the original Tarot cards as does the Bavarian *Tarocken*.

Eventually 'Tarocken' developed into a synonym for playing cards generally – and this fact again led many researchers to believe that the Tarot was the beginning of all card games.

In the mountainous cantons of Wallis and Graubünden in Switzerland, the traditional Tarot cards are used for playing a rather complicated game of Tarot. In the canton of Fribourg, a similar game is known, now played mainly by elderly ladies.

In the Engadin, however, the old Tarot game has been revived again in the last few years. The rules can be traced back more than 150 years, and the fact that natives from the Engadin never regarded the Tarot as divinatory cards supports our theory that there was no uniform development of the old Tarot.

TAROT AS A MEDIUM OF DIVINATION

When introducing the Tarot as a medium of divination, several basic considerations must be pointed out.

Without any doubt, there are things between heaven and earth which we cannot grasp rationally. There is also no doubt that we possess certain powers without knowing them ourselves. In our modern, technical world, people are becoming more and more prepared to consider media we can neither understand nor explain. From chiromancy to astrology, from numerology to the crystal ball – in the last few years, all kinds of predictions have happily been revived.

Obviously this development also carries some dangers. I would not like to introduce the Tarot cards as magical, but rather as a medium for getting to know yourself better.

The Tarot offers us a unique opportunity to think about the past, clarify the present and set up a prognosis for the future – all relating to each person individually.

I am not in favour of questioning the cards about a pools win or the next reminder from the taxman. Nor do I believe that one can read auntie's visit or the canary's death in the cards. Use the cards on serious problems. Make yourself ponder and analyse these problems thoroughly. This step alone will help towards coping better with life.

There are many indications that the cards can help. For a modern person it is not easy to believe that through shuffling the cards, the seeker's magnetic powers will influence their sequence to make up conclusive images and prognoses. Nevertheless, serial tests have shown that the main aspects do not alter, or only minimally so, even if the cards are laid out several times.

A second reason which might help in our belief is that Tarot cards have been read in very much the same way for 500 years, and that the interpretation of the individual Arcana has never changed. At least the fact that a game has remained unaltered in its meaning for such a long time gives reason to believe that a medium has been used which bears a unique truth, even if it was never fully understood.

FUNDAMENTAL INFORMATION ON READING THE TAROT CARDS

Right from the start, I would like to distinguish between the serious reading of Tarot cards and reading as a party gag. Of course, the latter is amusing and will help to make a social evening more interesting and entertaining. Especially in the United States, reading the cards has turned into a real party sensation, and has established itself in the social lives of young Americans.

If reading cards at a party, please do not take the cards seriously. Don't be tempted to interpret them in too much profound detail and don't forget that the main aim is to entertain and amuse the gathering.

Here, we will concern ourselves with the more serious way of reading the cards. There are a few points, discussed on the following pages, which you should not disregard.

We will begin with the people involved. The person who has a specific problem and is seeking an answer to it from the cards is called the seeker or subject. Of course you can read the cards for yourself. The normal procedure is, however, for the seeker to turn to a person who is knowledgeable in reading the cards.

It is important for the seeker to concentrate totally on their problem. There is no point in trying to deal with several questions or problems at a time. The seeker has to concentrate exclusively on the one, most important problem. This question is only rarely said aloud. Merely by concentrating on it and by using the image of the cards the reader should be able to read the cards. In most circumstances the reader must not know the question.

For me, it is important that the readings take place under four eyes only. Very often the cards will reveal a constellation of a highly private nature, and the reader might find it difficult to interpret the cards properly in the presence of an audience.

Use a quiet room when reading the cards. The seeker and the reader should be seated opposite or to the left of each other. The cards are arranged in their normal order, then the seeker shuffles them. Then they are handed back to the reader who will lay them out in one of the various possible spreads – two of which are described in the following pages – and interpret them.

Take your time when reading the cards. Work your way through, from card 1 to card 10. At the end, summarise your interpretations and try to avoid secretive gestures of hints to any impending disaster.

It is an advantage not to know the seeker personally. The reader could otherwise be too easily tempted to interpret the cards in the way he knows the person, and not as depicted by the cards. Unavoidably, however the reader's personal opinion will occasionally make itself felt in the reading. This, of course, drastically alters the value of the statements.

Every person who is prepared to read the cards should be well aware of the inherent responsibility. A nervous, frightened or obviously unstable person should never have the cards read. It is too great a danger that single statements will be taken out of their context, or that single images which at first glance might appear to be threatening, such as Death or the Devil, are taken too seriously. The reader must always be aware of the fact that the Tarot cards do not offer a ready-made prescription for the future, and that their real value lies in helping us to think impartially about our past, to thoroughly analyse the present, and to project the sum of these insights onto the near or distant future.

The reader should abstain from any kind of mysterious behaviour. The mere fact that the cards are being read for them is exciting enough for most seekers. There is no need to surround the process with much ado and thereby intimidate them even more.

It is very important that the reader really occupies himself with the Tarot cards; there is no point in offering the seeker every possible interpretation. It is the reader's task to set up a clear, definite picture into which, of course, the seeker's personality should be built. One can tell a good reader by the result, and the result should always be such that the seeker can draw a use out of it. Intimidated or frightened seekers generally point towards a bad, unprepared or immature reader.

As a reader, you will soon find out how exhausting

reading the cards seriously is. I would recommend no more than three sessions a day. A session takes about one hour, in which you have to be fully concentrated and be constantly aware of the responsibility you as a reader of the old Tarot cards bear.

The seeker should understand that it is useless to ask the same question more than once a day. He should concentrate on the result and try hard to draw some conclusion from it which is helpful and positive for his or her personality.

It is an old tradition never to read the cards for children but only for adults. Quite apart from the fact that children should be kept away from processes which are so difficult to understand, it is irresponsible to make an unsuitable attempt at interpreting a past which cannot, as yet, be conscious.

People who are psychologically confused should under no circumstances have their cards read. They would not be able to grasp the messages, and their disturbed emotional life would cause a likewise confused and unreadable spread.

I strongly advise you against reading the cards for your partner, husband or wife. It is extremely difficult to differentiate between your experience of them and the signs from the cards. Furthermore there are truths in the cards which you might not be able to tell a person with whom you are closely involved.

THE CELTIC CROSS SPREAD

There are quite a number of possibilities in spreading the Major Arcana. One of the oldest spreads, the Celtic Cross, is also the most telling one, and has the added advantage of being relatively easy to learn. The Celtic Cross spread is used mainly for answering direct questions.

Put the 56 Minor Arcana aside and order the Major Arcana according to their numbers, with the unnumbered card, the Fool, on top. Ask the seeker to select one of the cards from the pack that they feel relates to the question being asked. This card is referred to as the significator. Place this card in the centre of the cross.

Hand the remaining cards, face down, to the seeker, who will suffle them and hand them back to you to spread as follows.

Place the first card in the centre of the cross on top of the significator with the words, 'This covers you'. This card is interpreted as pertaining to the subject's thoughts concerning the question. It indicates his present position and gives us information on the situation in which the seeker is living, and on his personality.

Place the second card crosswise over the first card with the words, 'This crosses you'. This card relates to the problems the subject may encounter while dealing with his problem. It explains the influence from the surroundings to which the seeker is exposed, and it gives us information on the obstacles and difficulties which the seeker will come across in the very near future.

Place the third card with the words, 'This crowns you' at the top of the first card. This is the card of fate which gives us an insight into the near past and the present possibilities of the seeker. It relates to the spiritual help and guidance available, or a favour owed to the questioner.

The fourth card is placed to the right of the first card with the words, 'This is behind you'. It is the card of the past and the subconscious. It relates to the circumstances that led the subject into his present situation. From this we may draw conclusions about the past and about those problems which are momentarily troubling the seeker the most.

Place the fifth card below the first card with the words, 'This is below you'. It gives us information about those events and influences which shaped the seeker most in the past, and which formed his personality. These can be incidents from the near or distant past. It indicates the words possible outcome or problems pertaining to the question.

Place the sixth card with the words, 'This is before you', to the left of the first card. This is the card of the future and relates to the immediate future circumstances that the seeker must face.

These six cards are actually sufficient to give an exact picture of the seeker. The four additional cards are to help us to make these statements more precise. The cards seven to ten are used to lay a row from bottom to top to the right of the cross.

The seventh card reveals the inner attitude and desires of the seeker. It shows how he would like the problem to be resolved.

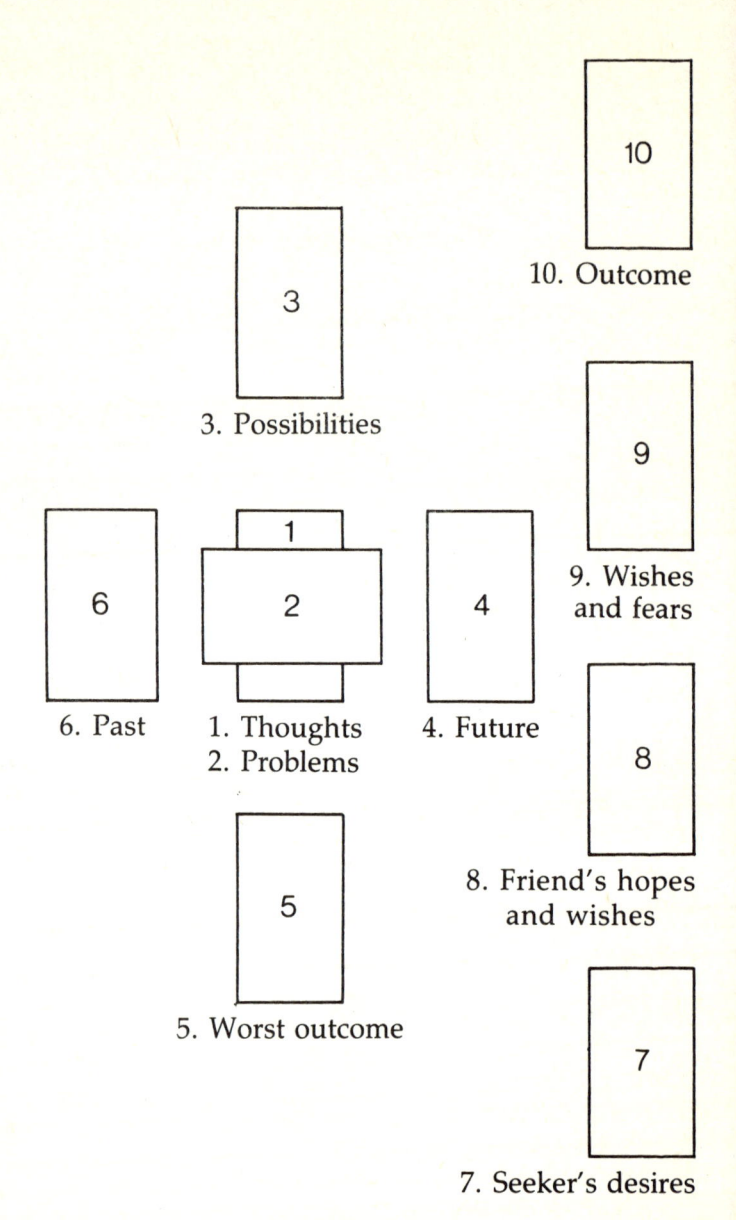

```
                                                    ┌─────┐
                                                    │     │
                                                    │ 10  │
                                                    │     │
                                                    └─────┘
                                                   10. Outcome

              ┌─────┐
              │     │
              │  3  │                               ┌─────┐
              │     │                               │     │
              └─────┘                               │  9  │
           3. Possibilities                         │     │
                                                    └─────┘
                ┌──┐                               9. Wishes
  ┌─────┐    ┌──┤1 ├──┐   ┌─────┐                   and fears
  │     │    │  └──┘  │   │     │
  │  6  │    │    2   │   │  4  │                   ┌─────┐
  │     │    │  ┌──┐  │   │     │                   │     │
  └─────┘    └──┤  ├──┘   └─────┘                   │  8  │
                └──┘                                │     │
  6. Past    1. Thoughts   4. Future                └─────┘
             2. Problems                         8. Friend's hopes
                                                   and wishes
              ┌─────┐
              │     │                               ┌─────┐
              │  5  │                               │     │
              │     │                               │  7  │
              └─────┘                               │     │
          5. Worst outcome                          └─────┘
                                                7. Seeker's desires

                   The Celtic Cross Spread
```

The eighth card goes above the seventh one. It shows the seeker's influence on his surroundings and gives us an insight into the problems the seeker experiences with his relationships, and how his friends and associates view his predicament.

The ninth card again goes above the one before. It is the card of the secret wishes and fears. The seeker's hidden hopes, fears, problems and uncertainties are expressed. The ninth card also indicates problems which might appear in the future.

The tenth card lies at the very top and represents the final outcome and the summary of the whole spread. This card should offer the solution and the logical explanation for the previous cards.

Now read and interpret the cards according to the interpretation of the individual images.

You will find the opposite meaning of a card explained as well, both for the Major and for the Minor Arcana. This occurs if a card appears upside-down. Interpreting the cards is obviously made slightly more complicated when adding this 'upside-down' reading, but as experience has shown, the outcome does not alter drastically. In any case, first try the easier version.

When using the more complicated method, place the cards face down and move them around, then hand the deck to the seeker for shuffling. As already mentioned, a card lying upside-down generally means exactly the opposite of the usual interpretation. However, don't forget that not only are the positive elements turned into the negative, but that the negative meanings become positive ones.

THE MAJOR ARCANA

Already after a few days' practice, the spreading and reading of the Major Arcana should be no problem. If you regard the individual images on the cards closely, you will soon realise that their explanation is obvious. The pictures talk and tell us quite clearly what they have to say. If you concentrate sufficiently on the cards' details and shades, you will very soon no longer need the instructions for interpreting them. The Celtic Cross spread is used to answer specific questions.

LE MAT – THE FOOL

The Fool walks along happily, light-heartedly, blissfully naive. His feet stand close to the precipice, but this does not seem to bother him. In his colourful, picturesque clothes he reveals joy, disarming naivety and serenity.

The Fool is the symbol for light-heartedness and especially for unconcern. Without being impressed by the world's dangers, he steps ahead nimbly, but also recklessly. His carelessness exposes him to many dangers which he cannot recognise.

Meaning

As its name implies, the card stands for foolishness, immaturity, unconcern and frivolity, thoughtlessness, lack of discipline, and unpredictable, imponderable behaviour, passion, and unreliability. The person drawing this card will have to invest a large amount of his or her energy in strengthening their personality and to give an aim and a goal to their life.

Reversed Meaning

If the Fool lies upside-down, he implies a standstill in life, disconnection and false happiness. The card can also point towards a wrong choice, be it the choice of a person or of a path.

LE MAT.

I LE BATELEUR – THE MAGICIAN

His gesture, pointing with the wand in his left hand to heaven, with his right hand to the table, symbolises all power coming from above. In front of him, on the table, are a whole array of objects such as boxes, balls etc., which are the symbols of the four elements. The magician has to put these seemingly scattered objects together to one whole object. He is to fill them with sense. The magician is smiling naively, but fairly self-confidently.

The observer will be amazed to see a magician or a conjurer with such a friendly, harmless smile. There is nothing evil about this man. Perhaps he is not even aware of his power, or has not yet found a way to direct it.

Meaning

This card stands for a strong and above all creative person. It symbolises spontaneity, imagination, self-confidence, originality, but also determination, self-control and a positive attitude towards challenges.

Reversed Meaning

Lying upside-down, the card means insecurity, delay, lack of imagination, directing one's energy into the wrong direction, unreliability.

I

LE BATELEUR

II JUNON – THE HIGH PRIESTESS

With a crown on her head, a strong stick in her left hand, the goddess is standing with bare feet on a wide road. She is dressed in a red dress, held together with a blue belt. Behind her, we can see a magnificent peacock.

Junon is the symbol of all female power, of the ideal woman. Wise and strong, capable of defeating the storm of the times, she looks into the future full of confidence. A woman or feminine force confident in her hidden knowledge.

Meaning

Junon symbolises understanding, intelligence, carefulness, knowledge, wisdom, responsibility and enlightenment.

Her clear mind and her profound knowledge are combined with benevolence and with understanding for mankind's weaknesses.

Reversed Meaning

Lying upside-down, this card stands for shortsightedness, egotism, stupidity, irresponsibility and ignorance.

II

JUNON.

III L'IMPÉRATRICE – THE EMPRESS

With the sceptre in her right hand, the left index finger threateningly raised, the ruler sits on her throne. Her head is adorned with a crown, her neck with two rows of pearls.

Meaning

The ruler means female resolution, fertility and efficiency. She stands for female relatives such as mother, sister, wife, children, as leader and as a businesswoman.

But she also embodies distinctly female characteristics such as loyalty, comradeship, discretion, economical consideration and lively interest in everyday matters.

Reversed Meaning

Upside-down, this card denotes lack of empathy, laziness, anxiousness, loss, uncertainty and bad luck concerning all women in close proximity.

III

L'IMPERATRICE

IV L'EMPEREUR – THE EMPEROR

The crowned ruler sits as a large, strong, bearded man on his throne. In the right hand, he holds the sceptre; in the left, his shield. His clothes, decorated with rich jewels, reveal wealth. His face expresses tranquility; he is aware of his power.

Meaning

The card of the ruler stands for power, worldly force, knowledge, ability, leadership and stability. It expresses stamina and resolution and symbolises the emotionless world of force. The Emperor is no sympathetic, emotional man but rather a 'doer'. He will succeed no matter what. He will attain his aims by whichever way the situations and circumstances demand.

Reversed Meaning

In this position, the card implies inability, unhealthy softness, lack of decision, of abilities and of stamina. It points towards a immature, soft person, unfit to cope with life.

IIII

L'EMPEREUR

V JUPITER – THE HIEROPHANT

Symbolised by a crowned, strong man with bare chest, Jupiter is sitting on a heap of rocks. His benevolent, bearded head is resting on his left hand, while in the right, he is holding a sceptre. An eagle is standing in front of the Hierophant, symbolising wisdom and farsightedness.

Meaning

This card stands for benevolence, sympathy, friendliness, for the art of forgiving and forgetting. It also depicts religious thinking, the readiness to serve – in short, for an emotional, reliable person who will any time take on a 'fallen person.'

Reversed Meaning

Lying upside-down, this card stands for exaggerated benevolence, impotence, untidiness, for a life full of difficulties with one's surroundings.

V

JUPITER.

VI L'AMOUREUX – THE LOVERS

Tenderly the young man is holding his lover's hand. Her calm, expressive face is watched closely by an elderly man who is leaning on a stick and keeping in the background. On a cloud above the lovers is Cupid, aiming his arrow.

Meaning

The Lovers express everything that is connected with love, beauty and harmony. This can be a passionate relationship just as much as a strong friendship. The card also symbolises each person's urge to discover and to conquer something new. It stands for passion, trust and honour. Family gatherings for happy occasions.

Reversed Meaning

Lying upside-down, the card points towards failure in human relationships, towards incompatibility of two people, a wrong choice, and towards the seeker's inability to share his or her happiness. It can also be an allegory for the disinterestedness with which the seeker regards his closest surroundings, and for the unconcern with which he pushes aside private and family problems. It can also indicate quarrels or disputes.

VI

L'AMOUREUX.

VII LE CHARIOT – THE CHARIOT

The warrior is standing proudly in his triumphal chariot. With challenge in his eye, armoured heavily, he faces the oncoming conflicts. In the card's bottom half, we can see the triumphal chariot pulled by two horses, each going in a different direction.

Meaning

This card means bad news, hostility, blows of fate or difficulties. But it can also stand for a change of place, be it travel or flight. It depicts triumph and greatness, while pointing out the dangers of too much success and popularity. The seeker very often is extremely superficial and too concerned with success. Eventual victory will be achieved when he finds his direction.

Reversed Meaning

This points towards failure, plans collapsing, towards rejection of insights, towards not wanting to accept reality and in the end towards desperation.

VII

LE CHARIOT

VIII LA JUSTICE – JUSTICE

This card can be number XI.

The female symbol of the main virtue Justice stands strong and fearless. In her left hand, she is holding Justice's symbolic scales, in the right, a double-edged sword which stands for power and decision. Justice is armed for every fight with her light armour, not prepared to accept compromise.

Meaning

Of course Justice symbolises justice, equality, virtue, honour and virginity, but she can also depict great self-righteousness. In any case, we are dealing with a strong personality who is capable of averting evil and doing good. This is a person who deserves our trust and who will never exploit our misery.

Reversed Meaning

Strictness, intolerance, obstinacy, also lawlessness and brute force, dishonesty and intolerance towards one's fellow men.

VIII

LA JUSTICE

VIII L'ERMITE – THE HERMIT

Seeking knowledge and truth, the hermit, clad in a brown robe of penitance, walks along. He is an old man. In his right hand, he is holding the lantern of the seeker – the light of knowledge.

Meaning

This card means silent knowledge, watchfulness, carefulness, but also closing up towards others, expressionlessness and emptiness. This card can stand for a person who is incapable of keeping up human relationships, but also for a tendency towards supressing emotions.

In any case, the hermit is a taciturn person who will keep secrets, a quiet, but very critical observer of his surroundings. He prefers his own solutions to problems.

Reversed Meaning

Lying upside-down, the card implies carelessness, recklessness and haste, immaturity, impatient, pointless activity and the inability to encounter one's surroundings trustfully. Can be socially inadequate.

VIIII

L'ERMITE

X LA ROUE DE FORTUNE – THE WHEEL OF FORTUNE

The Wheel of Fortune stands at the edge of a precipice, attached to stony ground. The female figure of an angel, blindfolded, is turning the wheel with eight spokes which shows how closely happiness and unhappiness, stability and change are linked together in the life of a human being. Whilst a young couple is sitting happily on the top of the wheel, a man is falling off it, tumbling into nothingness. A strong rose-bush is growing from the stony ground.

Meaning
The Wheel of Fortune is the wheel of fate. It stands for belief, success, result, for the solution of a problem, but also for change, for an unexpected event which is announcing itself.

The Wheel of Fortune queries the statements of the following cards and can change their meanings completely.

Reversed Meaning
This means a deterioration of a situation, bad luck, blows of fate, a person's own failure or unhappiness, and fear of change.

X

LA ROUE DE FORTUNE

XI LA FORCE – STRENGTH

With bare hands, a man of athletic build is taming a wild lion. Full of confidence and calm, he will succeed in this inequal fight. He feels so strong he doesn't have to revert even to the large red club lying in the foreground.

Meaning
This card stands for strength, for power of resistance, for strength of body and mind, for self-confidence and virility, for a sensible use of means, for energy and for overcoming evil.

Reversed Meaning
This implies weakness, pettiness, but also abuse of power, tyranny, indifference, and impotence.

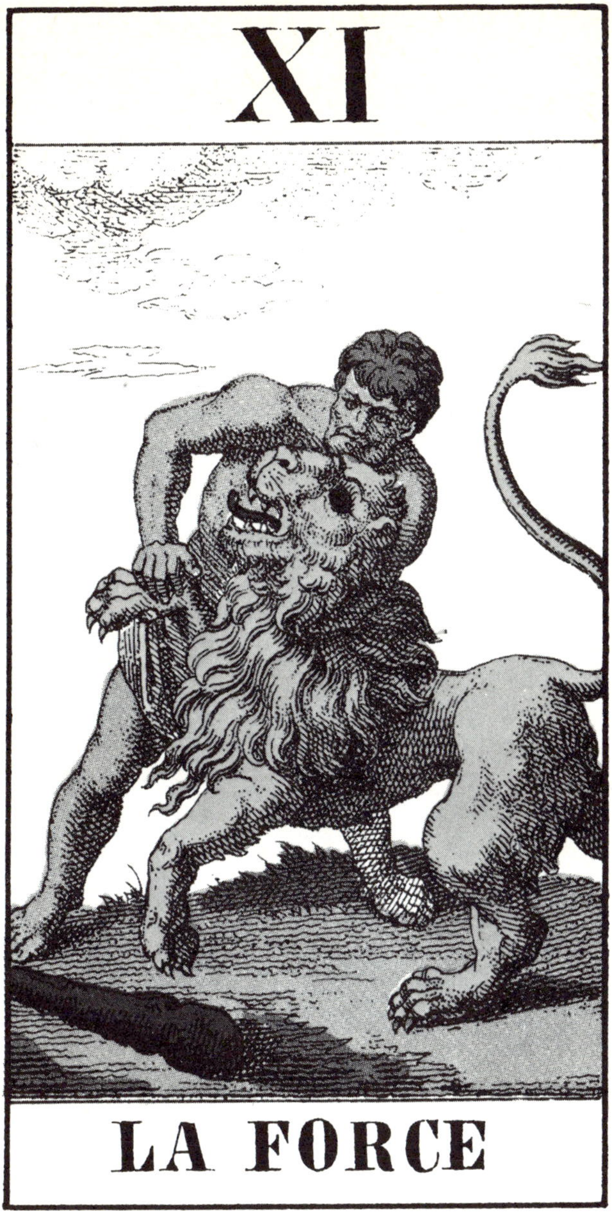
XI
LA FORCE

XII LE PENDU – THE HANGED MAN

The Hanged Man is one of the strangest cards of the Major Arcana. Tied by one foot, a man is hanging from a wooden beam which rests between two tree trunks. His right leg is bent backwards. His arms seem to be bound behind his back. Yet the man's face does not express pain or desperation, but rather tranquility and disinterest.

Meaning

The seeker has given up in his endeavours. He is 'drooping' in the full meaning of the word, is passive and listless. He will rather resign than use his strength to change his fate.

A second meaning of this card is re-birth, revival, a beginning, a new beginning, a complete re-think, a change in one's whole way of life, or a rest before action.

Reversed Meaning

Prejudice against oneself and others, insensible resignation, victimisation of oneself, life in illusions.

XII

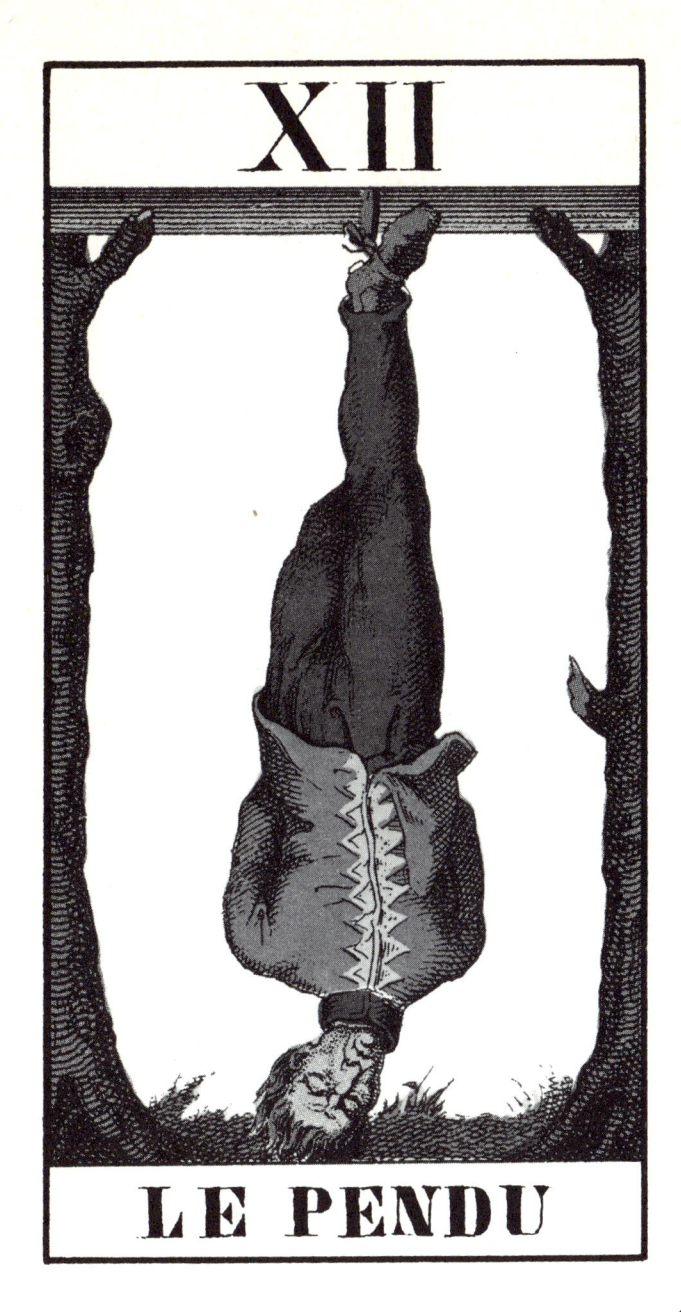

LE PENDU

XIII LA MORT – DEATH

Holding a colourful scythe in his hand, the skeleton stands in the centre of the page, seemingly cutting the stony ground. In the background we can see a small house, two mountains and the roof top of a large farm.

Meaning
Although the card is called 'Death' and bears the number XIII, it does not necessarily predict evil. It can mean illness, death, loss, collapse and disaster, but in most cases it points towards great changes which are taking place, towards a new beginning and new development in life. It can mean the end of difficulties within the family, or of family friendships. A change in everyday life, in financial security. In any case, Death is a card which wants to remind us of life's transcience

Reversed Meaning
Lying upside-down, the card shows recovery from a shock or an illness. It stands for immobility and idleness, for stagnation and for a quiet, even boring life.

XIII

LA MORT

XIIII TEMPERANCE – TEMPERANCE

An angel of strong build is standing at the edge of a river, pouring water from a brown into a red jug. The red jug has the shape of a hexagonal urn. The water symbolises the water of life. Along the river we can make out woods and trees. The angel and his strong wings indicate energy, security and perseverance.

Meaning

This card points towards modesty, self-control and moderation. The seeker is aware of his or her own limits, is both loved and respected, and this card indicates a happy future.

But the card can also depict lack of activity; perhaps the seeker is being too modest, too kind and too amiable to attain the success he or she is hoping for.

Reversed Meaning

Hostility, clashes between business and personal interests, inability to work in a team, unfulfilled wishes, frustration.

XIIII

TEMPERANCE

XV LE DIABLE – THE DEVIL

The figure with its horns and two-pronged fork offers a frightening and terrible sight. Standing naked, with a long tail and hooves, he indicates his power over all humans with his right hand. In front of him a woman is crying.

Meaning

The card does not indicate luck. It points towards slavery, resignation, towards subordination, perhaps towards black magic and sudden disaster.

The Devil, as symbol of death, unhappiness and poverty implies shock, brutal force, self-imposed destruction and evil influences from the outside world.

Reversed Meaning

Lying upside-down, this card indicates the first step on the way to perfection and to enlightenment. The fear of one's self has been overcome. The seeker is about to realise that any kind of subordination and slavery can be overcome. There are no obstacles which cannot be removed.

XV

LE DIABLE.

XVI   LA MAISON DE DIEU – THE TOWER

A mighty building, similar to a tower, is being destroyed by lightning which seems to come directly from the sun. A man is falling head over heels onto the yard, where a second man is already lying. Everything is crashing into the street – whole parts of the tower, wooden beams, stones. The lightning of truth is destroying the construction of lies and bias.

Meaning

This card stands for complete collapse of old relationships and traditions, for loss of friendships, for a total change in one's view of life, for disruptions, perhaps even bankruptcy.

In any case, it means loss for the seeker, be it a loss of security, of love or trust. As positive aspect, this card points towards a breakthrough to new times, to new possibilities.

Reversed Meaning

In this position, card XVI, too, suggests a boring, motionless and monotonous life, the seeker's complete inability to give new impulse to his life, even possibly a bad and unpleasant situation in which the seeker is finding himself.

XVI

LA MAISON DE DIEU

XVII L'ETOILE – THE STAR

A young girl with bare breasts is kneeling at the edge of a lake and is pouring water – the giver of all life – back into the lake, using a yellow jug. Above her is shining the star of hope, surrounded by four golden and two other stars. These stars symbolise new happiness which is appearing, whilst the water stands for man's ability to learn. Falling stars indicate hope and a promising future.

Meaning

The Star is a card of luck, revealing belief, hope, insight, optimism. It points towards the stars' influence at the time of our birth, to the fact of any astrological influence.

This card means fulfilment and reward in our efforts, contentment and pleasure.

Reversed Meaning

In this position the card denotes unfulfilled hopes, disappointment, useless relationships, unsatisfactory business and an unbalanced character, both inwardly and outwardly.

XVII.

L'ÉTOILE

XVIII LA LUNE – THE MOON

In the top half of the card we can see a young man who is serenading a young girl on a balcony, playing his lute. A big, strong dog is sitting next to the man. A round, child-like moon illuminates the picture. The crayfish seems to be wandering straight up to the moon without paying the slightest attention to the young lovers.

Meaning

The card of the moon brings bad luck. It shows disappointment, insincerity, dishonesty, bad influence, tricks, cunning.

The card in any case indicates that the seeker is in danger of making mistakes. He is exposed to new, unknown influences which might lead him into dangerous, risky situations. Perhaps he is prepared to turn somebody else's misfortune unfairly to his own advantage. The card may also hint at extremely insecure relationships or at unknown enemies.

Reversed Meaning

Lying upside-down, the Moon card indicates that the seeker is capable of overcoming temptations, avoiding mistakes and realising dangers before the damage has been done. Even in this position the card reveals that the seeker is exposed to unhealthy influences, but it shows that he is capable of mastering the inherent dangers.

XVIII

LA LUNE

XVIIII   LE SOLEIL – THE SUN

A large, vigorous sun is shining above a harmonious, happy scene. Two lovers are sitting in the foreground, clasping each other tightly, with an open book in their laps. The strong sun seems to have conquered the dangers of the stars and the moon.

Meaning

This card is one of fulfilment and success. It stands for love, for joy and dedication, for a happy marriage, for happiness on earth and happiness in everyday life. It expresses both the contentment in devoting oneself to others and the expectations of a close friend.

But it is not only a card of triumphal happiness. It can also express contentment, for instance the ability to accept life as it has been pre-ordained, without the seeker reverting to idle passivity.

Reversed Meaning

Again, this bears the opposite meaning – failure, bad luck, abandoning plans and projects: a dangerous time which holds many losses.

XVIIII

LE SOLEIL

XX LE JUGEMENT – JUDGEMENT

The angel Gabriel is sitting on a cloud and is sounding his red trumpet for the Last Judgement. A woman and three men, clad merely in light blue clothes, seem to have risen from their graves. Doomsday, the day of rewards and the day of terror, has broken.

Meaning
The moment in which we have to account for our lives is near. The card could mean that our way of living presents a big problem to other people. Inexplicable processes are taking place in our minds. The seeker tends to solve problems without considering his fellow men. The card of Judgement promises success to those who are open and honest towards themselves.

Reversed Meaning
Separation, divorce, missed chances and delay; a life lived in fog, a life without light and clarity.

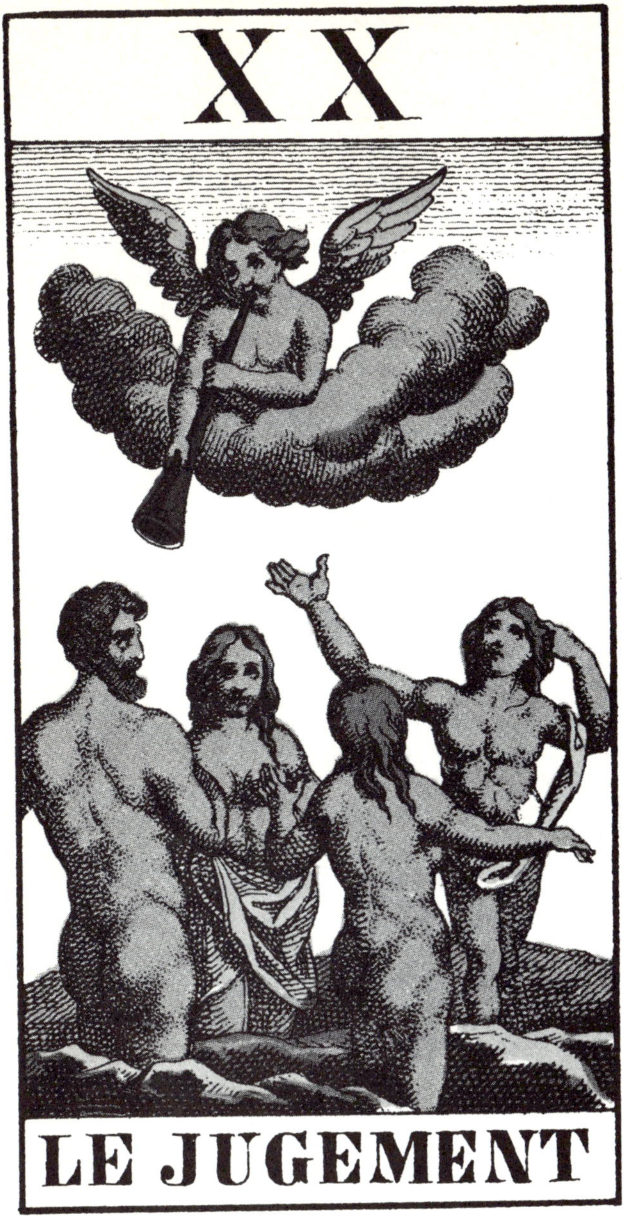
XX
LE JUGEMENT

XXI LE MONDE – THE WORLD

A naked female beauty, holding a blue shawl in her hands, symbolises the joys of the world. She is surrounded by a wreath of colourful flowers, with a watchful eagle perching above her. Protectively he is spreading his wings over Mother Earth. The two birds to his left and right help him in his watch. In the bottom half of the card there are an ox and a lion protecting the female figure.

Meaning

The world stands for the fulfilment, the conclusion and the final result of all our efforts. It shows that we are about to succeed in what we have been aiming at.

Being the strongest and the most significant card, it takes effect all by itself, but influences every other card. Its main significance lies in a positive, satisfying and happy conclusion.

Reversed Meaning

This stands for imperfection, for fear and disappointment and for the inability to realise our plans.

XXI

LE MONDE

THREE SAMPLE SPREADS

Having explained and read to the seeker the individual cards according to the preceding interpretations, you will now deal with the relations between the various picture cards. These relations can be of great importance, and the complete sequence of the spread may indeed reveal a very clear trend.

In the individual interpretations, I already pointed out those cards which are especially strong, i.e., whose significance bears greater weight. However, there can be no reading by mere categories of 'strength'. The reader will use his or her imagination and common sense. If you, for instance, find a strong image like the Sun next to two negative cards, it is quite obvious that the sinister aspect of the preceeding cards is at least weakened.

When reading the cards, it is important to study the relations between those cards which affirm or support each other. For instance, in the final interpretation, the cards I and VII must be seen together; likewise, cards IIII and X will simplify reading in the future if read in close connection. There are also always connections between cards IIII and VIIII, although these ties are not necessarily as obvious as with the other mentioned pairs.

It would go far beyond this book's limits to try and describe the impact of each card on all the others. But with a little practice and thought every reader will soon find out how the complete image is made up and whether it is coherent. The three following examples and their interpretations will give you a good introduction into reading a spread of Major Arcana.

MARY M'S READING

The seeker is a highly individual young lady between 25 and 30 years old. She is married and works in an office.

In position 1 we see the Devil. The card indicates that the seeker is experiencing an extremely unsettled stage of life and being confronted for the moment with heavy personal problems, restrictions and limitations. It would be wrong, however, to interpret this card in too negative a way, as we can see immediately that its impact is weakened by surrounding cards.

In position 2, we find card number XIIII, Temperance. It shows us that the seeker is trying to adjust to a new situation. Perhaps she is as yet not putting enough energy into this.

The Star in the position of fate, position 3, shows that the seeker recently went through a happy period and that she strongly believes she is steering towards a positive future.

In position 4 we can see the Emperor. In earlier years, it was a male person who most formed the seeker's being, and now, again, it seems to be a man who is the problem. It might be that the present male differs too much from the earlier image of the man, especially regarding strength and determination.

The Empress in position 5 indicates that the seeker's life was also formed by a strong, benevolent woman. This woman was not necessarily a dominant personality; she could have been an exemplary character.

The Sun lies in the future position. Everything points towards a happy and contented future. However, to attain that it is necessary to accept life as it is predestined.

The Moon in position 7, just like the card in position 1, shows that the seeker at the moment is going through a difficult phase in life. She seems to be exposed to very strong influences which might get her into dangerous situations.

Although the Moon indicates insecure relationships,

the reader should beware of announcing this immediately as an existing or threatening crisis in marriage. Often it is only minor and seemingly unimportant problems in some human contacts that are being hinted at, and the breaking off of a relationship does not necessarily always relate to the dominating person in the seeker's life.

The card in position 8, Strength, again reveals problems with the surroundings. For the people around her, the seeker is very strong and self-confident and apparently always feels it necessary to use her means sensibly to avoid greater difficulties.

The Wheel of Fortune in position 9 explains inner wishes and problems. Again we are told that something is happening, that changes are emerging which already showed themselves in the positions 1, 7 and 8.

The Hermit in position 10 reveals the solution to all problems as being solitude and reserve. To attain a happy goal, it is important to observe the surroundings critically and to make an effort to keep up relationships. The seeker must take care not to shut herself off too much from the people around her.

CYNTHIA B'S READING

The seeker is an emotional person who gives a cheerful and rather relaxed impression. She is not married and works in a responsible position. She is between 25 and 35 years old.

Card number 1, the Fool, reveals a cheerful and easy-going personality, perhaps as yet not quite fully developed. There seems to be a certain inclination to act unpredictably and to 'live for the day'.

Card number 2, the Magician, seems to express the problem fairly clearly: the seeker is confronted with a very strong personality who apparently shows more self-confidence, more determined self-control and also more courage when faced with everyday challenges.

The third card is Junon, the High Priestess. She hints at a life which passed happily and tells us that the lady in question is trying hard to overcome her defects and to show responsibility and understanding towards her fellow men.

The Empress is in position 4. She reveals that the seeker's main problems in the past – and perhaps still today – lay in the contact with other women. The Empress's strength implies that these were people with extremely strong determination, whose claim to dominate may have caused problems to the seeker.

Le Chariot in position 5 hints at blows of fate and at difficulties that had to be mastered. It shows that a change of place or a journey must have been a major influence.

In position 5, as card of the future, we find Jupiter. He hints at introversion, at a development towards being a very emotional and reliable person who can show benevolence and sympathy.

The Lovers are in position 7. Apparently the seeker is very much in love, or at least bound in a very strong friendship. Passion, love and the search for harmony are playing a very big role at the moment.

The eighth card is the Emperor. It is remarkable that it is the strong, domineering men who prevail in this spread. We believe that the seeker is influenced by several strong personalities. This influence is not necessarily bad, but the seeker's emotional life often receives a blow from these hard personalities.

In position 9 we can see Justice. She tells us about the

seeker's secret wishes which all are concerned with justice and strength. Although she has a fairly distinct personality, she secretly continues to look for further balance, for levelling her often weak character.

Do not be irritated by finding the Wheel of Fortune in position 10. We can deduce that a change in the seeker's life is imminent. Taking into account the preceeding positive images we believe that this change (which is not necessarily imminent but may take place within the next twelve months) will be a change for the better.

73

WALTER M'S READING

The seeker is an efficient, successful man in his forties. He works as a managerial executive, is married and has three children. The man gives the impression of being slightly nervous and makes no comment on his problems.

In position 1 we find the card XV, the Devil. The seeker is in the middle of a crisis. One can surmise that he is exposed to restrictive influences from his surroundings and that his greatest problem is not being able to fit into a certain order, and accepting the fact that he is a subordinate only with difficulty.

Card number 2 is Death, confirming the impression we gathered from card number 1. And indeed, things seem to be changing. The card may mean that certain difficulties are coming to an end, or that a friendship is terminating. But the change may also occur in financial matters.

With the Star in the position of fate things look a lot more positive. The momentary problems will be overcome and everything will find a happy ending, if he puts his plans into action.

Judgement in position 4 tells us about the seeker's past. Apparently his problems were connected with his rather reckless way of life. Without wanting to, he might be a real trouble-maker. His fairly bombastic character often offends the people around him.

The Sun lies in position 5. The seeker comes from a happy home. He has a quiet, orderly youth behind him and grew up in surroundings that had a positive outlook on life. It is, however, possible that he may have been spoilt too much, so that he is now inclined to withdraw into unhealthy passivity.

Justice in position 6 shows that the seeker is heading

for a bright future. He will develop into being a person who deserves the trust of those around him, who will always try to do good, to stand up for fairness and to fulfill his duty. It is obvious that this in turn may lead towards an inclination for self-contentment.

Card number 7 is Temperance. At first glance, there may seem to be a discrepancy between position 1 and position 7, but we can read from that that the seeker's main problem is his lack of activity. Often he is too uncertain, too undecided to actually achieve the success he could have. More often than not he doesn't come up with the required effort.

In position 8, we find the Fool. Very often the seeker presents himself to his surrounding as slightly foolish, immature, flippant, perhaps even frivolous. This exaggerated jolly behaviour with which he portrays himself leads towards being judged wrongly and causes problems in his career.

Jupiter, as a strong card, in position 9 symbolises the seeker's inner wishes and problems. He would like to regard himself as being strong, he tends towards thinking in emotional terms, is even inclined towards religion. Being humane, friendly and kind means very much to him, but this also causes difficulties in the present way of life.

The Wheel of Fortune appears in position 10. As we have seen with cards 1 and 2, everything with this seeker is 'on the move'. Changes will take place. The seeker will give up his restlessness and attain the goals he is aiming for in the foreseeable future. It is very important that he heads for this goal with great consideration and prudence in order to regain tranquility.

DISCUSSING PROBLEMS

After reading these three examples, you might be wondering which specific problems these three people had. I, being the reader, will never know, as a discussion on the actual problem should not take place, not even after the reading. Otherwise you will only too soon to take on the role of being confessor and will burden your own emotional life with problems which are actually none of your concern.

The more you delve into the seeker's world of problems, the more difficult it will be for you to read his or her cards the next time. It requires nearly super human efforts to concentrate so hard on the cards so that there is no space for personal projections and considerations.

THE MINOR ARCANA

Some spreads include the Minor Arcana so it is useful to study these and learn to understand their meaning and significance. The Rows of Seven spread is explained in the next chapter.

The Minor Arcana consist of 56 cards. For the beginner it might at first seem impossible to understand and remember their individual significance. Therefore don't hesitate to look them up whilst performing your first readings, and don't try to interpret the images from emotional intuition alone. One thing, however, you should try to learn immediately: the main tendencies of the various suits; you will need to be able to grasp their significance at a glance.

Once you've learnt to recognise the images and their respective categories, you will be able to tell with a glance at the rows of seven, towards which complete image the spread is tending.

Swords	Air	Ideas	Strength, courage, force, activity, battle, sorrow.
Wands	Fire	Energy	Work, progress, development, growth.
Cups	Water	Emotion	Emotion, pleasure, joy, happiness, unions, relationships.
Pentacles	Earth	Practicality	Possessions, money, wealth, possessions.

SWORDS

The suit of Swords represent strength, courage and force. They are the cards of active people who enjoy engaging themselves – not only for the good, but also for evil. It is the suit of the commanding and the fighting spirit.

Significance

King of Swords
Supervision, command, strength, activity, justice and conclusion.

Reversed meaning: Love of power, wickedness, unscrupulousness, sadism.

Queen of Swords
Grief, poverty, defamation, separation, loneliness.

Reversed meaning: Faint-heartedness, malice, treason, revengefulness.

Knight of Swords
Heroism, forceful impulse, leap into the unknown, movement. This card has a great influence on the surrounding cards.

Reversed meaning: Stupidity, lack of responsibility, inability, quarrel, conceit, immaturity.

Page of Swords
Attentiveness, watchfulness, inclination to inquisitions,

recognitions and revelations.

Reversed meaning: Deceit, possibly illness, clumsiness and helplessness, as yet undeveloped.

Ten of Swords
Grief, sorrow, tears, unhappiness, disappointment, pain and illness.

Reversed meaning: Material gains, success, progress in financial matters.

Nine of Swords
Quarrel, difficulties, unhappiness, broken heart.

Reversed meaning: Fear, scruples, defamation, shame.

Eight of Swords
Revolution, uproar, imprisonment, terror, crisis.

Reversed meaning: Blow of fate, unforeseen events, negative experience, deceit.

Seven of Swords
Hope, trust, new outlook on the future, efforts, imagination.

Reversed meaning: Hesitation, trembling, bad advice, quarrel.

Six of Swords
Conquering the unknown, overcoming difficulties, road, travel.

Reversed meaning: clarifying an unsatisfactory situation, frank discussion, confession, seeking in vain for a solution.

Five of Swords
Conquest, destruction, victory, nastiness.

Reversed meaning: Danger threatening people close to the seeker, insecurity.

Four of Swords
Seclusion, loneliness, convalescence after an illness, postponement, standstill.

Reversed meaning: caution, energy; if acting cautiously, the situation will improve.

Three of Swords
Separation, loss, absence, loneliness, delay.
　Reversed meaning: Restlessness, confusion, mistakes, loss.

Two of Swords
Health, harmony, love.
　Reversed meaning: Lies, dishonesty, falsehood.

One (Ace) of Swords
A great wish will be fulfilled, joy, success, possessions, perhaps debauchery.
　Reversed meaning: Force, resistance, destruction, bad luck.

WANDS

The Wands are the suit of the working people and the craftsmen. They represent work, progress, development and free enterprise.

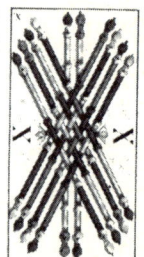

Significance

King of Wands
Congenial, amiable person, friendly and responsible, wealthy, intelligent.
　Reversed meaning: Weird ideas, not open to reason, a pushy and obstinate person.

Queen of Wands
Desirable woman, charming and attractive, understanding, honest.
   Reversed meaning: Infidelity, flightiness, jealousy.

Knight of Wands
Travels to unknown countries, departure and absence, journey by plane or by boat.
   Reversed meaning: Termination of a relationship, sudden change, disruption.

Page of Wands
A messenger, a stranger with good intentions, a friend; trusting and reliable.
   Reversed meaning: Insecurity, cowardice, messenger carrying bad news.

Ten of Wands
Stress, problems, overstraining, misuse of energies.
   Reversed meaning: Threatening loss, deceit, dishonesty, intrigue.

Nine of Wands
Troubled times ahead; secret enemies, problems.
   Reversed meaning: Grief, enmity, worries, delay.

Eight of Wands
Restlessness, haste, unhealthy speed, lack of thoroughness.
   Reversed meaning: Misunderstandings, jealousy, strife, unpleasant discussion.

Seven of Wands
Victory, triumph, material gain, professional success.
   Reversed meaning: Doubt, fear, hopelessness, no prospects.

Six of Wands
Glad expectations, reward, happy ending, things are moving.
   Reversed meaning: Waiting, distrust, fear, dishonesty.

Five of Wands
Discord, efforts, stress, quarrels, destruction.
   Reversed meaning: Efforts, action, enmity, deceit.
Four of Wands
Harmony, tranquility and happiness, deserved reward.
   Reversed meaning: Unsatisfactory relationships, restlessness.
Three of Wands
Proficiency, enterprising spirit, clarity.
   Reversed meaning: Dishonest helper, false friends.
Two of Wands
Strong personality, determination, leader.
   Reversed meaning: Surprise, grief, worries, loss, relapse.
One (Ace) of Wands
Conception, birth, beginning, gain, perhaps debauchery.
   Reversed meaning: Insecure future, bad prospects, decline, resignation.

CUPS

The suit of Cups represents emotions and religion. The cards show joy, pleasure, happiness. They promise fulfilment and happiness.

Significance

King of Cups
Knowledge, wisdom, high-ranking personality, artist, advisor, trust and responsibility.
 Reversed meaning: Dishonesty, debauchery, temperamental, scandal, loss.

Queen of Cups
Adored, beloved and loving, generous and sympathetic, honest and trustworthy.
 Reversed meaning: Unreliable, liar, double moral standards.

Knight of Cups
Suggestion, appeal, invitation, conscription, belonging to somewhere.
 Reversed meaning: Theft, tricks, an unpleasant, dishonest person.

Page of Cups
Sensitive person, clearsighted and obliging, thoughtful.
 Reversed meaning: Easily influenced, unconcentrated, flippant.

Ten of Cups
Happy family, middle-class virtues, happiness, homeliness and joy.
 Reversed meaning: Family strife, friendships are lost; unhappiness, resistance.

Nine of Cups
Material wealth, success, victory, good health.
 Reversed meaning: Material failure, loss, misused trust.

Eight of Cups
Inhibitions, fear, disappointment, insecurity.
 Reversed meaning: Festivity, joy, happiness, success.

Seven of Cups
Wishful thinking, the world of dreams, illusions.
 Reversed meaning: good choice, willpower, the goal is coming closer.

Six of Cups
Childhood, memories, past impressions, happy remembrance.
  Reversed meaning: Changes are coming, plans cannot be realised.

Five of Cups
Futile relationship, marriage of convenience, loss, sorrow.
  Reversed meaning: Hope, new connections, old relationships will revive.

Four of Cups
Hostility, trouble and worries, fear and disappointment.
  Reversed meaning: New approach to solve old problems, new revelations.

Three of Cups
Solution to a problem, good results, compromise.
  Reversed meaning: Uncontrolled debauchery, loss of esteem and prestige.

Two of Cups
Passion and love, being in love and marriage, old friendship.
  Reversed meaning: Problems in love and friendship, separation, termination, perhaps divorce.

One (Ace) of Cups
Joy, happiness, beauty, fulfilment, complete devotion.
  Reversed meaning: Unreturned love, bad friends, restlessness and change, coldness.

PENTACLES

This suit belongs to the merchants. It symbolises money and therefore the impulse and driving force for every business activity. It refers mainly to financial matters.

Significance

King of Pentacles

A mature, strong personality, calculator, experience and success, strong character, determined.

Reversed meaning: Corruption, unscrupulous, disbelief.

Queen of Pentacles

Magnanimity, mercy and generosity, security and wealth, luxury and comfort.

Reversed meaning: Neglect of duties, fraud, credit, debts.

Knight of Pentacles

Patience, tenacity, stamina, insistence, responsibility.

Reversed meaning: Aimlessness, purposelessness, standstill.

Page of Pentacles

Crave for knowledge, learning, thoughtful and studious.

Reversed meaning: Without logic and reason, no realism, rebellion.

Ten of Pentacles

Family, happy life, home, security, wealth.

Reversed meaning: Gambling, loss, risks, bad news.

Nine of Pentacles

Love of nature, caution, reserve, trust and discretion.

Reversed meaning: Possible loss of a relationship or of a precious possession.

Eight of Pentacles
Position at work, training, modesty and honesty, effort.
Reversed meaning: Intrigue, pettiness, lost claims.

Seven of Pentacles
Money, gain, possessions, progress, growth.
Reversed meaning: Loss, caused by rash dealings and careless, investments.

Six of Pentacles
Benevolence, gift, generosity, gain.
Reversed meaning: Jealousy, egotism, financial troubles, debts.

Five of Pentacles
Male or female friend, emotion, loss, poverty and worries.
Reversed meaning: The situation will improve, new possibilities are opening up.

Four of Pentacles
Materialism, stinginess, pettiness, narrowmindedness.
Reversed meaning: Problems at work, set-back, dismissal.

Three of Pentacles
Strength, popularity, musical abilities, success at work.
Reversed meaning: Money problems, laziness, bad work.

Two of Pentacles
Problems, resenting new projects, worries and trouble.
Reversed meaning: Letter, sudden unexpected success, joy and happiness which are not quite true.

One (Ace) of Pentacles
Aim, wealth, fulfillment, treasures and works of art.
Reversed meaning: Loss, possession without luck, health is threatened.

THE SPREAD ROWS OF SEVEN

In America, there is an especially old spread called the 'Gypsy spread'. I do not know how much of a connection exists between this kind of layout and the fortune-tellers. However, if you wish to try this layout, this is how it is done.

Remove the 22 Major Arcana from your deck and put them aside. Shuffle the 56 Minor Arcana and take the top 20; the remaining 36 Minor Arcana will not be needed.

Hand 22 Major and the 20 Minor Arcana to the seeker and ask him or her to shuffle them well. Then, face-down, the seeker lays the cards into six piles with seven cards in each, putting them down one after the other from right to left. Now the reader picks up one pile after the other starting with the first, and places the cards, face-up, in six rows from right to left.

A male seeker is portrayed by the Fool, the Magician or the Emperor; a woman is represented by the Fool, the High Priestess or the Empress. Whichever of these three cards appears first when being laid out is removed and placed to the right or to the top of the first row of cards. The empty space is filled by the top card from the unused pile of 36 Minor Arcana.

Row 1 reveals the past. Experiences and impressions which played a major role in the seeker's life are depicted here.

Row 2 describes the present. Everything that is affecting the seeker at the moment comes to light in this row.

Row 3 shows the influences from other people, social pressures and stress at work which all lie beyond the seeker's grasp.

Row 4 reveals the near future. Combined with the results from the preceeding three rows, this row will indicate the main tendencies and movements which the seeker will be exposed to in the very near future.

Row 5 hints at future possibilities. Here we can read what the seeker can do to avert any inconvenience and to build up a successful future.

Row 6 shows the goal and the result. From this row the reader can tell which result the seeker can – and will – achieve.

Row 1: Past | 7 | 6 | 5 | 4 | 3 | 2 | 1 | P

Row 2: Present | 7 | 6 | 5 | 4 | 3 | 2 | 1

Row 3: Exterior Influences | 7 | 6 | 5 | 4 | 3 | 2 | 1

Row 4: Near Future | 7 | 6 | 5 | 4 | 3 | 2 | 1

Row 5: Future Possibilities | 7 | 6 | 5 | 4 | 3 | 2 | 1

Row 6: Goal and Result | 7 | 6 | 5 | 4 | 3 | 2 | 1

THREE SAMPLE SPREADS AND THEIR READINGS

Once you have laid out the cards in the manner described, you start reading them from right to left. If the reader goes about this task prudently and intelligently, an exact picture of the main streams in the seeker's past, present and future will be revealed. Do not deal with each card individually, rather take in the image of the complete row.

The Major Arcana are always stronger than the Minor Arcana and therefore strongly influence their significance. The overall picture of the Rows of Seven spread is nearly always determined by the Major Arcana; the Minor Arcana's main function is to support and clarify this picture. However, if there is only one Major Arcana in a row, the Minor Arcana's significance will, of course, gain greater weight.

The following three examples will give you a few hints and some information on how to read and interpret the Rows of Seven.

The 'personality card' next to or above the first row helps you to gain a general impression of the seeker's personality.

PAUL F'S READING

The Layout (from left to right)
Row 1: XI, XII, V, XIIII, King of Wands, VIII, Ten of Swords.
Row 2: Ace of Wands, Seven of Wands, VII, III, Ace of Cups, Four of Cups, Six of Swords.
Row 3: II, Three of Wands, Two of Wands, XVIII, XV, Eight of Swords, XX.
Row 4: XVI, Two of Pentacles, Nine of Swords, Four of Wands, XIII, X, XVIIII.
Row 5: King of Cups, Six of Swords, Three of Pentacles, XXI, XVII, I, VIIII.
Row 6: Nine of Cups, Eight of Cups, VI, Ace of Pentacles, Fool, Page of Swords, Five of Cups.

The Interpretation
Mr F introduced himself as an artist. He is about 45 years old and very difficult to fathom. He exudes a certain restlessness, an irritated tension.

Past
The cards XII and the Ten of Swords tell us that the seeker experienced some heavy blows of fate in his youth. Illness, even an ailment troubled him. VIII, V and the King of Wands draw the picture of an intelligent, kind and sympathetic person.
These characteristics made life easier for him in his youth. Cards XII and XIIII reveal that apparently softness, passivity, and laziness were the seeker's weak points.

Present
The seeker's current situation is confused. The Six of Swords in position 1 however hints at an overcoming of

the problems; Ace of Cups also promises success and is supported by the Seven of Wands. Card III shows a strong woman helping towards forcing the breakthrough. Card VII illustrates that blows of fate and his enemies' actions will continue to hit him. The seeker suffers from his fear (Four of Cups) and tends towards intemperance (Ace of Wands).

Exterior Influences

This row reveals a very clear picture as nearly all cards denote dangerous negative powers. XX hints at difficulties with the surroundings, the Eight of Swords speaks of crisis and unrest, XV and XVIII mean injustice enmity, and dangerous influences. The seeker urgently needs the positive powers from the Two of Wands, the Three of Wands and the High Priestess to be able to counter what is happening around him.

Near Future

Cards XVIIII and X promise success and unexpected solutions, XIII changes, and the Four of Wands a reward. So the seeker is on the right path. The Nine of Swords, the Two of Pentacles and the XVI predict that this turn for the better will not take place calmly.

Future Possibilities

This whole picture looks very good and shows that the change announced in the previous row will take place. The seeker will gain a good position on a musical and professional level, and his efforts will be rewarded by a positive ending. This we can see clearly from cards VIIII, I and XXI which are supported by the Three of Pentacles, the Six of Swords and the King of Cups. XVII does point towards unknown enemies, but their importance is diminished in the whole context.

Goal and Result

Once the seeker has broken off the final worthless relationships at which the Five of Cups in position 1 hints, he will live in wealth and peace. He will overcome his insecurity and inhibitions (Eight of Cups). His connection with the arts and his inclination to discover the unknown, indicated through the Ace of Pentacles and the Page of Swords, will help him lead a joyful, unburdened life. This happy future is revealed in the cards the Fool, VI and the Nine of Cups.

Success will come from a liaison or partnership which will allow the subject to grow beyond the realms of the Fool to the completeness of the wish granted by the Nine of Cups card.

SIMON K'S READING

The Layout (from left to right)

Row 1: Two of Cups, Eight of Swords, Page of Wands, V, Queen of Pentacles, XVIIII, X.

Row 2: III, Ace of Swords, Nine of Wands, Four of Cups, Page of Pentacles, Eight of Pentacles, XXI.

Row 3: Ace of Wands, Two of Wands, I, VII, VI, King of Wands, IIII.

Row 4: XVIII, Nine of Cups, Seven of Swords, VIII, XI, Six of Pentacles, Eight of Cups.

Row 5: XIIV, Nine of Pentacles, Five of Pentacles, Queen of Swords, VIIII, XII, XX.

Row 6: II, XIIII, Seven of Wands, Nine of Swords, XVI, XV, XVII.

The Interpretation

Mr K gives a happy, balanced and self-confident impression. He is a person who loves company; he finds it difficult not to talk during the reading. He is about 40 years old, an engaging, well-groomed personality.

Past

The seeker spent a protected childhood and youth which shaped very much by a kind, wise father and an especially close friendship. His somewhat fervent emotional life seems to have led him into a crisis which he overcame, however, without major difficulties. The seeker obviously is a very social person in whose past especially, friendships played an important role.

Present

Although the Nine of Wands and the Four of Cups reveal that not everything is at its best, the seeker seems to be going through a relatively happy phase of life. In his profession, he has succeeded in attaining his goal. He has been rewarded for his efforts. There are no financial worries, and he also seems to be happy in the family sphere, though he has hidden fears.

Exterior Influences

The seeker is exposed to the influences of strong personalities, which for the main part however act positively on him. His surrounding encounters him with trust, but also with love. His healthy self-confidence and his originality have earnt him an interesting and large circle of friends.

Near Future

The Eight of Cups and the Moon signal a few problems in the near future, but the positive aspects by far outweigh them. The seeker will continue along his advancing path, with success showing itself especially in the consolidation of his personality.

Future Possibilities
Life will not remain as wonderful in the more distant future. Painful changes will make themselves felt. Card XX, however, shows us that the seeker will realise the threatening problems in time. He will consider his situation and, after a phase of emptiness and loneliness, of renunciation and failure, he will find his way back to his path of success.

Goal and Result
The subject should break away from restrictions and put his own ideas and plans into action if he is to obtain the dream of the star.

A decision must be made in the cycle of a moon II (the High Priestess) if the balance is to be achieved.

MALCOLM R'S READING

The Layout (from left to right)
Row 1: Five of Pentacles, XI, Ten of Wands, King of Wands, Six of Cups, Eight of Wands, II.
Row 2: Page of Cups, Ace of Cups, XX, Ace of Swords, Nine of Swords, Eight of Swords, Four of Wands.
Row 3: XVIIII, Seven of Wands, Knight of Swords, VII, VI, XXI, XVI.
Row 4: XVII, I, XII, XIII, XIIII, XVIII, X.
Row 5: IIII, III, Four of Swords, Knight of Wands, Nine of Pentacles, Four of Cups, XV.
Row 6: Page of Wands, VIII, VIIII, Two of Cups, V, Eight of Pentacles, Nine of Cups.

The Interpretation
The seeker is a sportsman, highly emotional, about 45

years old. He strikes one as being successful and charming, but one cannot but notice a certain restlessness within him.

Past

The seeker's adolescence was dominated by a father who was extremely authoritarian and who often demanded too much from his son. As a result, stress and inner restlessness appeared. Despite happy memories of his childhood, the efforts and worrries dominate.

Present

The seeker suffers from a broken heart. The Four of Wands indicates a flirt, the Eight of Swords upheaval and crisis. We deduct that he is not sure about his emotions and therefore is faced with several problems. The Page of Cups reveals the seeker to be an emotional person, which does not alleviate matters. But from a glance at Row 2 it is obvious that the difficulties lie within the emotional sphere, and not at work or in financial matters.

Exterior Influences

This row to the greatest extent confirms what we already saw in the preceeding row: restlessness is around. XVI even indicates collapse and loss. The most important card in this row is VI. We can see the lady who is causing the seeker so many problems. Judging from card XVIII, everything will turn out well.

Near Future

Many things will change in the seeker's life; the Moon next to the Wheel of Fortune, Death and the Hanged Man all point towards that. A sinister stage of life is approaching, in which the seeker might fall into passivity. It is uncertain whether an illness, at which the card XIII hints, will play a part. The Magician and especially card XVII improve the picture. They suggest that the seeker will be strong enough to get through this difficult phase of life without greater damage.

Future Possibilities

The negative aspects from Row 5 are confirmed here with the cards XV and the Four of Cups. The Knight of Wands indicates a long journey, and the Four of Swords promises convalescence from an illness. A strong, kind woman will help the seeker overcome his depression, and card IIII explains that the seeker can manage the situation due to his knowledge and his intelligence.

Goal and Result

Throughout the spread, there always is a strong positive card in position 7. These hopeful final cards in each row are confirmed in the whole row 6. Despite his success, the seeker will not hold back emotionally either, as the Two of Cups indicates. The difficult experiences from the past caution him towards being more careful and perhaps even cutting himself off. On the whole, however, the result is a positive one, both in regard to material and to emotional matters.

Justice causes him to be wary of others and protect his own interests, the Hermit following with Two of Cups shows he wants to share his life and needs to find someone he can trust sufficiently. The High Priestess shows a future relationship will bring both financial and emotional security into the subject's life.